FELONIES OF ILLUSION

also by Mark Wallace:

Walking Dreams: Selected Early Tales (BlazeVox 2007)
Temporary Worker Rides A Subway (Green Integer, 2004)
Haze: Essays, Poems, Prose (Edge Books, 2004)
Dead Carnival (Avec Books, 2004)
Oh Boy (Slack Buddah Press, 2004)
The Monstrous Failure of Contemplation with Aquifer by Kaia Sand
(self-publish or perish, 2001)
My Christmas Poem (Poetry New York, 1998)
Nothing Happened and Besides I Wasn't There (Edge Books, 1997)
Sonnets of a Penny-A-Liner (Buck Downs Books, 1996)
In Case of Damage To Life, Limb, or This Elevator (Standing Stones, 1996)
The Haunted Baronet (Primitive Publications, 1996)
The Lawless Man (Upper Limit Music, 1996)
Every Day Is Most Of My Time (Texture Press, 1994)
Complications From Standing In A Circle (Leave Books, 1993)
You Bring Your Whole Life To The Material (Leave Books, 1992)
By These Tokens (Triangle Press, 1990)

FELONIES OF ILLUSION

Mark Wallace

EDGE

Cover and typesetting by K. Lorraine Graham

Some of theses poems were first published in the following publications: *Antennae, Bridge, The Capilano Review, Combo, Hundreds, The New Review of Literature*, and *War and Peace 2*. The author would like to thank the editors.

ISBN 13: 978-1-890311-26-1

Edge Books are published by Rod Smith, editor of Aerial Magazine, and distributed by Small Press Distribution . Berkeley CA * 1-800-869-7553 * www.spdbooks.org * order@spdbooks.org

Edge Books * P.O. Box 25642 * Georgetown Station * Washington, DC 20007 * aerialedge@aol.com * www.aerialedge.com

Contents

THE LONG REPUBLICAN WINTER

1.

                                        to talk about
                                        machines
                                        or what is not
                                        machine

          is to be them or beyond them?

                         stuck
                         and the cloudy sky
                         above the river freeway

                              *

          balled
          into a tight
          protective shell

                                   maybe argue them out of it

                              *

                    "every apartment
                    has identical features"

                              *

     work hard
     and money owns you
     work less hard
     and money owns you more
     as in, money owns you

                              *

                                    on loan
                                    in the cut rate light

                                    organization
                                    insinuation

                                    the way to the top
                                    pale rider

                    *

all this halfway
not so poor as

freedom means
someone's got it worse

2.

inhale
exhale
walk out
release the arms

keep the back leg
in contact with the earth

*

a calm
here   detonation
before

*

sure
a fight seems
just right
tonight

*

in the name of a solution

3.

you're in demand
but there's no pay

the street arc
of the self available

                                                *

                                    pulled him
                                    off the bus
                                    then opened the windows

                                                *

            sarcastic
            images of the agent

            feel better?

                                                *

                                                            one to go
                                                            one more to go
                                                            there's only one more
                                                            and maybe one more

                                                *

do this
that
this
that
this
that
just do it

                                                *

too many
to fall from

the quiet
moments of trouble

*

Sing me now
a political song
of how the poor
will one day be free

Sing me now
a political song
that'll bring the bloody
torturers down

Sing to me now
of what will be
because all I know
is I can't see

Sing me that song
and make me believe it
because I don't know if I can

4.

take a Monday
off to catch up

the little things
and their big agendas

remainders and distraction

*

the promoter
and the law

sing hey diddle diddle
the cops come down

to haul away
illegal profits

a fire sale
boats guns and cell phones

"all money goes
for your protection"

no one knows
the story behind it

they just like the song

*

the network
of blood connection

webs out
through electrical pulse time

a sense of home
helps lower the rate

don't let the kids
go out without the signal unit

*

                                        congratulate yourself
                                        after the emergency

*

one assertion another breakdown
hearing what you wish they were saying
about who's lost in your ruffled purity
to be unfocused a condition of nothing
and the folks at the table know you don't see
the way you're falling again

*

            ten minutes
            for poetry

            so good
            today

            to not be dead

*

                                        all the bodies
                                        gathered

                                        here for cocktails
                                        only a few squeeze in

*

trying
to describe
things
on the square
when the cubicle
has no windows

*

unknown name
unknown number

has your name
has your number

rings at 5, 6, 7,
rings so you buy

a machine to detect
a machine then detected

struggle in the wires
for pulse and pulse

a certain fee
makes sure no one's there

*

the market
and the bodies

the music
from ice-clogged streets

no way
to be remembered

*

it's not been this cold
since the last invasion

*

the boy loses the girl
it's fall in the park

that's the story he knows

apparently it's just a rumor
about the rest of the world

*

Friends come over
it's Wednesday and ice
gathers on the windows
we play Captain Beefheart,
Zoot Sims, Syd Barrett
note that the corner
liquor store has closed
we talk about poems
and parties on the weekend
we have lives we want to live

Outside, the US military
prepares to bomb Iraq

6.

how many
days a week
do good things happen

record weather (cold)
guys fighting on the lot

and the bulletin:
hey Mark, we like you
and will help

just when I thought
I knew everything

7.

plan to live on a mountain top
to fix cars in a town
to not have to take
anyone's bullshit anymore
thinking to replace it
with your own

*

row of lights
on a building roof
and I imagine traveling

*

what about seditious boredom

*

if you don't like your job
look inward
and find another job?

existential careerism
offers self-love discounts

help yourself help
the business along

lovers needed
for bomb manufacture

*

most
countries have them

some
use them

*

                                        red brick tower
                                        smokes
                                        against the sky

                        *

                static electric
                for a moment
                casing the fusebox

                                *

falling asleep
in a borrowed office
wanting to go
deep down

                                *

                a thug kills a thug kills a thug kills a thug
                and a lot of us too

8.

The lecture stated
how best to live

no one asked me

"the world is a lie
and we are the liars"

dull throb
winter and a job to do

that's the advice?
get the money and go?

someday
will never be this day

and this day
is what I've got

9.

traffic jammed
in all directions

I walk home easily

*

The Washington Post
says
what The Washington Post
wants other people
to hear it saying
says
what it says
to be what it is
says it for millions of dollars
hard to beat
a deal like that
and call the whole thing news

*

all this snow
and the shouting

(and the bullets
and the wakes)

*

fast track to free

*

get your duct tape
your gas mask
stay indoors for fear
of what floats on the air

*

                                        people come in
                                        go out again
                                        all that movement
                                        headed around

                    *

if I get the last word
what happens next

                    *

          they would kill you
          so you kill them first

          you would kill them
          so they kill you first

          they would kill you first
          so you kill them before that

          you would kill them before that
          so they kill you even earlier

          and before that etc
          shoot the kids

                    *

                    as for Tex-Mex
                    I'd rather skewer a burrito
                    than gag on the chains
                    of well-connected watchdogs

                    *

                                        say what you want
                                        say what, you want

                    *

the logic of war
builds a coffin

the logic of anti-war
rushes a fence

people killed
for the most boring reasons—

the way the others talk about living
leaves the chains intact

10.

helicopter overhead
sirens and sirens again

people march and carry signs
others sit in sun on the circle

frequent honks
send no clear meaning

a moment seems poised
then gone

*

definitions by which
"something happened"

definitions by which
"you didn't change the world"

*

hey you with the orange hair
and bulbous clown nose
stop walking under the bucket okay?

11.

> pale clear sky—
> thin white clouds
> trace where airplanes flew

*

> heard the audience
> boo and cheer
>
> the newspaper claimed
> the audience booed
>
> lying now
> even in things hardly noticed

*

an exercise in logic—

> A bombs B,
> B bombs C,
> says, "They started it."

*

> I want to sleep
> tonight beside the one I love
>
> I want to be indoors and warm
> I want to eat and drink
>
> I want work that matters
> to speak with friends
>
> I want music and games
> to walk in sun, wind and rain
>
> Is it really that much to want
> that so many should be denied it?

*

I walk downtown
then drive to the suburbs

everyone accuses
someone else's injustice

spring sun comes
through still bare trees

all these people claiming light
is that why they can't see

12.

it would be wise to want
nothing from the human world

let my wisdom fail me

*

reporters
embedded in the army
would be smart
to like the army

*

after the words
of the quiet poet

my hands twist,
scuff cracked,

ball themselves
against balance

*

work here long enough
you'd start trading poems for jobs

money doesn't ask
how you'd like to have it

the poet who doesn't need a job
meets a worker who doesn't need poetry

they stare at each other and neither can say
what it takes to live in the world

*

show how the world's complex
the audience says they don't get it
make it simple
no one hears it that way either
tell people they have eyes
they'll say they can't see you
then one moment deep at night
a body flies awake and stares

13.

illness and position papers
accumulating paper cups

*

the rising price of real estate
hasn't defeated poetry

walk the street after dark
steel beams are inspiration

*

it's a shame to have no lightness
to boom and stomp, to be this sunk,
to stand and want to fall

*

sun and stars
didn't plan this battle
neither did anyone I know

the sense of our lives
ripped off by thugs
we don't meet and wouldn't want to

to make as art
shell casings left
after the tanks drive off

where monument and rubble
finally have traded places
people kneel and start to build

14.

the winter's gone away

not the world stuck there

*

       pink flowering trees
       new light green leaves

       the cross and the chapel
       remember nothing

       people walk past
       showing off skin

       bells ring the time
       and no one stops

       why not admit
       how much is here

*

              the question
              could be answered with names

              the names
              have positions

              the positions
              determine other positions

              freedom
              is a maneuver

              the mind rebels
              running to nowhere

*

           one day I want
           to make nothing happen

*

save the scraps

*

Donald Westlake says

"polemicists
write about politics

novelists
write about people"   (Book World, April 20, 2003)

leaves me wondering
where politics comes from

*

forgot the things I meant to say

*

eight weeks
of cough and sore throat

unable to talk much
or like people either

snow and ice gone now
it's sunny and warm

people dead now
who writes about them

stuck indoors and sick
I don't even know who they were

*

in today's atrocity...

FELONIES OF ILLUSION

Ride

To ask how the hand blunders through.
When half-trained reserves come out
we haven't heard the word. Could be zippo
jumps to number one, or here

misses number ten, the beach at number eleven.
Just trying to kill some big name time
and took a deep breath, hot and beat
drink loads of water. That's all

to twist through an effect
downwind the cost of a cell phone.
Issued a warning of psychological
weather served with crackpots.

We don't have time to get stuck
so we do on purpose. Notice
who doesn't the long way out.
Call it someone's past on a penny

with the best guarantee in the business,
no bugs, hassles or sex.
What's the next event to wait for?
Buy now and pocket shiny

earth turned info stove top, hasn't been
any for you if you were none
steel reinforced. A little security
in an insecure truck. Guys?

Parked

Subversive, profane, iconoclastic, crude
rituals of personal appeasement staffing

don't have no bully pulpit to plunder
the next fanatic locust son.

Despite the tantalizing blame,
North America stands for broken

gun rebuttals; do you wish
to withdraw cash? Terror of the hailstorm

becomes proverbial working girl
apart from doing it over again.

Have a water bottle included, ounces
measured historically, tie-ins

to a refreshing age-of-lying tale
with access to teenage tonalities. Distribution

goes against, finally hears the call,
fully intending whatever it steps on.

Work Me

Dust off your subordinate
clamor referrals. Illustrious tear-free side dish
wrings the body straight,

solitude and companionship
wrecked on a float, ain't that right
my nervous Cheetah? Flaunt the dearth

welcoming the White House, we've stolen
this cartoon before. No one loves
the fool who mentions the labels.

Sick so you wave your hands
in the wit someone has about them,
ashamed of honor in the lapse

stuck discussion. Call security.
Did you seize photocopied irregular
goners like artificial wildlife

heads into smoky deep-rem sleep?
Something to do all fucking day.
Death is driving the powerful crazy.

Stop the season's premiere entanglement
in dramas that tell you what you're thinking
each time the long haul keeps on hauling

neural nodes' blunt hurt. Tonight
has no circular mind erasure, seed-belted
or crusted on machines

that must be mistaken. As opposed to there,
here is where you are, some say,
do you see the lovely house I live in?

Photos From Abroad

Castle and sandbox, interleague
craps hoot madhouse you're inside
miscues rattling down the road
delusions unfurled. You've come a long

hacked trap. Hawaiian real estate
not withholding loss or gain
in patented technique, what about
the people on the 39th floor?

Incredible no spill brain caps
offered in the best condos going
thereby leave top bugging systems
posing as heads of state.

We've got a shuttle launch to make
fooled scrunching, a comment
on why we're not home? A shine will counteract
unforseen last minute additions

of another lofty advancement ritual
for pilots too conflicted to fly.
Familiar harrowing transportation,
faked love and a frog in glass,

silly fluke to stake a career
on reports of heavy cheese.
Call it an adventure say.
Contact whoever's left to forget

side by side American sky deals
spinning in a first rate bubble,
two by two abandoned satellites
in the shadow of an international incident.

Enjoying Time Off

Institute no vacational rectitude
among the pool chairs, Reggie,
for time bounces proper faults

the speaker blows back.
Would futile fibers bother the brain?
Not so many as nail it in.

Did I tell you what darkness curls
cleft undone alone in bedrooms?
Who exactly looked there?

I was just sticking the ground
a vast rope around, wonderful well
to dig out of a bank job,

hard working funny friends
as an official first act.
Jam the flack against a call

which stalls the world and its peoples.
I don't know to know you do I.
The find you make is happy

for one bright canticle molecule,
two spins on a sculptured avoid
having done drowned an idea good.

Not Around Here

Flat backed to add, platoons prime
the empty drill. Fork over nerve blends

as family hoards. Nobody could say.
Start thunder cities labeled project.

Morning moons, anti-monopoly referrals
like to walk the little dog

some smaller than of. Who'd it go.
Charred in an aisle where silence

could sit still, rumors erupt in sixteen
astonished juveniles, loud, frenetic

and visually startled about one sudden loaf.
Nor endangers the sink to loan.

Doesn't fornicate a prudent menace
among drum solos. Called a bugbear

blunder and bluster. Longest odd slacks.
Show lesser ladders falling as perspective's

set in the updated present. Standard
dry public jackhammer kisses

lead one purge to another. Past no apology
drama heaps. The room, I mean.

Picking up a booty call? Appreciate
new dwellings where tacked revised

giveaways at this time
compose quick sliver kick backs

toned on turned, foiled under famous names
felled there. Curl basic old map disguised.

Barter

New indecision's breakdown backdrop
won't let me go to the store beside
a terminal discrepancy, I love you
and you love power and I become power
but really specifically, like a dollar bill
or a lost loaf of bread. Total hand
carries itself, bricks say to walls.
Sugar's a good combustible head end.
Do you like poets or being one
earned refuge, check out those shacks.
Should we do Survival Island
and stake an emblem? Flustered.
Call a shift to not be home
under a renegade special effect.
It's exactly not to be barking about
all the mud in the honey. Some silence
just ain't worth its hogwash.

If The World's Neurotic, What Am I?

Big night and bigger problem.
If decay can turn to comfort
we can't even feel delinquent,

spite and slice extravaganza
managed by a manager.
I see dead people.

You don't have to hide
lots of cash on a fluke
spear or ruin, shuttle

one more time to displace
my part of the general sandwich.
Why am I following me?

There goes my identical
freakish coincidence quit cold turkey
behind the pillar, which way

love is strapped to the tracks
with all the body gifted
to uncover the hottest story

so I get this mail. Wonder
who will be sentenced longer
to grow like an international system

doing what it damn well pleases.
No one wants my product.
Cruise a major traffic headache.

Filling The Weekends

Where'd the urgent tale get lost
documenting some latest con game

all over one more floor.
Who's so stand as list is searched?

18th annual bluer than blue
non-sequitur teetering, any chance

of having your dreams downwind?
No one drowns to want anymore.

Zipper, stair and refrain
beside rapacious mood swings

part along a catastrophe
and reflection's insomniac call backs.

Tell me how to be there before.
Span a future farmer, contrasted

wildly with age. Another mumbled anthem
huddled in a back seat binge

will learn to be copped romantically,
basement nightmare light fields hidden

and a way that might as has to go
tumbles all shambling roots.

A Question Of Semantics

No waiting for lots of speed with lots
of surface. Just when the blender
began to mix day to day

dilemmas and delusions, we noted
the ascendant profit motive flipped
repopulating the earth.

It's exciting to roll on these pillows
and watch the televised high speed car chase
in a room that's more to our liking

than the cops who speak well of lost
product hordes. Don't slam
the lid of night on the anger

that's not afraid to face mechanical
lessons about the first good thing
to shut us down. Whatever you say,

what are the conditions for believing
it to be expressed that way? I object
that our objections are not the object.

Our Best Intentions

Maybe you should take
quality cheer freshening

on videoed backdrop
ultimate fantasies finally

in charge.
What was certain

after a routine
test bubble dynamo

specialist who sees
night go different?

Tell them you won't
accept less first

story blue
nothing farces who

seek the mystery
man. Who'd like

to fund now impossible
items in the blinking

city? Happy
blockage doesn't get

licked on air
play plastic spoons.

Let's face it we're
no friends of environmental

aids to grow
whatever takes two

small shots a day,
high rate nonsense

per minute moisture
tremors take off.

Don't Buy Furniture

How hard can it be
to save eight bucks at the official
clown face, not to mention

mass sales of children's products
provided you've got pictures.
Can you see what can see

looking back attacked apartment
window surfing illusional toss
family comedy bit? Visual suspects

clamp down on tetrahedron
small change maze plays
that turn around and tell everyone

you've kissed the wrong bomb.
I don't know which door won't open
to demand recovery dated

by times to shoot the gun.
Will you excuse the night once more
for not defending the outpost?

Here To Help You Through

Do you know what a pound of mechanics
costs excuse not being a waiter
expert skills that turn against us
and now diehards are stopping

handy autodidacts? Your connection
left for another universe, can I get you
the small packed bills? I want someone
who does something for me

with yarn. We should have read
the warnings and been welcome to pay or weep
in typical timed response. Could you teach
reciprocal laundered number frames

no more than one at a time?
Toss down moribund jacks?
Settle the Jamestown Colony
with a hectic rematch? Put them together

yourself they burn less, let's eat
to echoes of the dark shift's
subtle chuckle. That was not
an incident. It's like the mother ship

calling us home to make a living.
Everything you see is poker.
When the door slams on my recalcitrant
monkey's the same as recommends

giving the air another try. They did it.
Don't miss a second of down home thrills
wrapped in an extravagant zest
freshly made, chasing a bottle of aspirin.

Really

Dropped in a legendary stew
I tell people secrets. Unemployed

sickness shoots up, trying
to figure a way to fall through;

thanks for the lights, gagged like a voice
that says nothing ever happens

during a mistaken reflex.
You should see the dark come down

so fast we find ourselves apart,
show time strapped to a function.

Lack In Buckets

Fallow hydrogens, convivial speckled retreads
and evangelical misnomers
catapult all time, love, and memory

while tough guys re-enact old wars.
The piled bags, towed and downing
daiquiris, share complexities of small town

hoeing on the glitter. Seals sell well.
Love's not leased where litter whirls.
The courage and the attic. Think you've seen

two heads resemble one? If the secret's
high strung and self-mismatched. Never as.
New identical towers demeanor no good or ill?

Like rock stars show a jolly walrus
keep bohemian distance. Advocated sublimes,
easy chair nuts and bolts. Who loves

a doomed sensational middle class suicide?
Causes like to sit. Paradoxical in background,
never doubt stranglehold emotions;

hospitals stir the strangest trifectas.
Let's never not as one, might wound not.
Nor more lonely in a drunken umbrella.

Send That Over Here

This tidal face explores
back bedrooms wrong with feeding

other fancy subliminals
and spin whomever casually.

Turn up the will to appreciate
per hour an old-fashioned hero

whose secret is don't bother.
Please I'd like to be lost.

When a bender high-tailed rocket
thinks even less than first expunged

everyone here wears band-aids
and becomes determined minor poets

among second-hand apocalypse
and mountain bikes. You would.

How'd you get those tattoos?
Hounded your own reflection lately?

That exactly I walk thrown back
to say who's never known to live

I'll break myself on anything handy
or otherwise known deprived as purpose.

Bubble

A mass in arrangements, a mask
strapped over a fusebox
a moment of lost
innuendo, hurt what hurts first.
Disturbs not so much what's
not to be, shouts in back rooms
because no one's listening.
Had intended to resemble
a dubious downcast upstart
cast out of every error
receiving first rate funding?
That's not how I meant
to say you away. Go so long.
There's not to know too much.

Random Behemoth

Strident bookcase flourishes latest
compact phone booth. Residual personality

calls the on screen number, mixing blow
when they hit it slowed. Here we

go again. Refrigerator truck sees
how you're doing, old joint sandbag

bright stun moisture, look up
awfully darn close direction by Sunday.

Who'll contaminate a wit around a shower.
Their blue ribbon ink with pride.

Because of his blip quality receiver
one kid has a problem. Catch some

to make all proud low prices.
Three European ambassadors hit.

Is this the feudal dumping ground?
My love can roller blade with the best

crazies on the rage. Is that gargoyle
ten bucks for former members?

Romanticism And Wall Mart

Now that you're working at new last cash
let's invite dogma, shut days down
cast beside dad in commercial chatter

who's outmaneuvering who?
Switching company phone bonanzas
and hanging up while others talk

about fresh air, here's a little
sample alphabetical list.
Nowhere's in this together nowhere.

I got iced at the restaurant
audio throat. It's cold
in the fake collection discussion

narrowed down to call backs.
Waited this long for repeatables?
Keep throwing the ornaments out there?

800 gallons of apartment
remorse refunds, get the door
as a way of going out it.

We'll see who eats asbestos and soup
better on camera films a quitter
daily caught denying the party

no one registered part of.
That's a mighty multi-value longing
for someone to kiss the cart away.

Dimmer Switch

I'll push you away to be
lost face spied, a sidewalk crunched

time to go to train for
speed. Troubled times splash

last moneyed legacy kills
pretending music I'd play

to bring you out of me
no more for any ache,

any fake of who cares when
skies go down ignored

reflections naming yours
mine breaking with dark

random turned down phones
speaking nowhere, a good

hook where you been
and throw away. Never mind

that we'll never see us
and want to not want.

Which Books Would You Bring?

Deserted on a survival expert
glued in a swimsuit heirloom
no no it's light to know at all
climbing while fingers get bloody

and toss out tales we touched.
The furniture melted into bodies.
Keep cool in acting storage rooms
(waffle irons, suits and poison)

do you think that basement's a man
working hard to communicate
like bigfoot with an axe? Who'd you fog
after time in the dark? What's with

a little bit of cremation for free?
Death is fashion. Careening edges missing,
knocked and moving, a choice
to be first in last year's fur.

Laughing at the happy candy
hanging at the coffeehouse with toads
or other corporate infestations
I thought dodos were extinct

in high-low jackpots. Today all day.
Help I want to be done showing up.
What's the best thing wrapped around you
glamorous at the end of a wall

enforcing so many judgmental snaps
tapping out the song. I think I understand
why I lost those chainsaws in open air
and put an image together again

to need to feel I feel talked backed to
when every mile counts on down
in people falling apart together
with captioned trust on cable.

New Misdemeanors

Can't get rid of love to be back
in a little chilling off. One of the world's
most endangered repair jobs fiddles

the window lock. Clear on out
in synch with hovering helicopters
officially undeclared. At the courthouse,

having lunch, no one's getting any
credible maneuvers and who's the woman
without a current reference nameplate

whence comes the jeep. Six jeeps, in fact,
circling a fountain, do one thing and do it
in a well that wants it black

what job got you, Joe? And on your left
a carnivore. Can you pronounce
guess what? Suddenly we're the surrogate

greatest gift, an offer, a tale
told for somebody else. The first time
might be the time to keep like crazy

one handle on a drive away loaner.
It's really right there right now,
the talk, the deal, the next game level.

Spray Day

It's happened before or every other guest
aches to be buried the new right way
proofs are proofs? When we set out to design
compact thinking, we ended up with lots

of transit to the usual beach spots
splintered on assumptions. Are you talking
to your hand yet? Out of signs,
tumble switched, thrown on

a presupposed interior call field?
Before anyone can toss in the towel
on top of excessive numbers or nightmares
read the instructions carefully. So does it

take ammonia? Could one highlight film
recall a bandit on the run
for all new greed? People are people
like news is gossip. Whatever I did

becomes equivalent border patsy
stressful reflex. If responsibility accepts
another slanted chain of events
to slip away from, the clamp

on the clamp, the public note,
slander advancement eats alive
at many a local hot spot, previewing blunders.
Step right up to the pressure cap.

Parallel Habits

I'm routed by your stamp knocked
profundity as ointment. Relentless asides

caught us on some funeral trial, plastered
like a recommended approach. Reliving one part

of the obfuscation. Married asunder.
Will you come back to me as pieces?

A linger calls the bog, open to disaster.
A sortie after singles, demonstrated via

videotape in court. Billions of consumers.
Rocked back so heels strike air.

Whereas under the wall generally liked it,
separation anxiety, my place on appeal

turns the chairs over in a pool.
Vacuumed doubts pose deployment risks,

inadvertent facial scrapes, psychoanalytic
plunder stuffed in mini-vans.

I'm lost without sold harnessed thumbs
and the note as a starved crash mutual fund.

Lacking Clarity Lately

A comedy about love, loss and other
eventual detours resembles
what you least expect. Think we've got

enough task fumbles? Cheap and close,
these prices raise betrayal
continuation expenses. It means

acting again. To work out friendship
with the evil twin, stretch the hours
and order three if you're hungry

enough to drown in it. Cut a hole
and just start pulling, your basic
hook in the bad news aisle

trying to add and looping around
before the breakout. Grab
whatever it takes and go.

Spurned House

Indefatigable night. How are
those handshakes full of tricks

and we would not be? Decline to fall
on a bed sheet surrogate asunder

too many you say I don't like
to be touched a responsibility?

Where does one go around
no carnival love diseases.

Write on walls or the arm.
Could one still wander as more than two.

To go to the store and represent
how the present fabricates

a multi-stop future hunting
pictures of slender muscled bodies

in a flight house cinema
dark to cake it on.

As no more than one
furrowed on a can't look back

to be what never was
more than misled to a borrowed screen.

Any Publicity Is Good Publicity

Won't have to testify about
pigs guilty on the rotunda. Get packing
nomad street misunderstanding

in second gear. Catch today
impersonating tomorrow. Down under
phone static, what's worth

being a cleaner health inspector
not wearing a hat? Screwed
on the cola marriage circuit

and the power's up for gripes
about who calls who.
Show me your badge again.

When it's time to shut everyone down
belted in the fort, the gala
credits go nowhere without

last minute invitations to fall
between the pinned down bars
and never seen industrial footage

of life replaced by lessons.
That's an excellent price to crash on
when manipulated by portions.

Daredevil

Time to tour the need to trade
one dead end for elaborate displays

and be careful how you mistrust.
A repeating spectacle splayed to the bone

lowest I can't believe, not allowed
we thought we had illegal exotic

poor little creatures in jail.
It's curtains if you knock on the door

yet can't fix the registration
fervor that would help us out

paging everyone's potential
with room for five, or choose the silence

in the show that must go down
in flight around the usual neighborhood.

Cooking Habits

Why is anything out for a reason
leaving the oven on? A provocative
lesson about speculation

becomes a hindrance binging.
I won't try to disappear
towards comfort over intervention

failing a seismic shift
one might have alone as rooms
depend on how to forget.

The Small Things

Luckily there's a corner that has
one corner left to hide. Broken car

against a lead post, an unretrievable drop
ties each street's impacted shadows

bundled up at cost. Half of these completed
stares define what's this from that

found naked in the cuts. Roll away.
Where's the nearest hot cost sleep clinic?

Call the scattered crash in pieces
the day that each new Rome starts to fall

on the necessary cry. Charts describing plutonium
leave us looking like faces at faces

while stratified recombinant theses
organize a futile trial

of impostors' lucrative undertow
that throw us groped at awe's refusal

down at the local bar.
I hate my regular clothes, you know.

Under Another Layer

Envy makes a totter reluctant
to bother the century off the night
that no one makes a love drug of,
trips to be lost taken out

about the most important time
of ludicrous reverse replaced
absolutely never round and round
regular or decaf death

on that stick? Best warranty
funniest action slap
for a second straight year-long
drought there was touching

you were doing here? Is that a problem
despite palpable tension
to crack the code and controlling
bossy when cut

by a person who trusts a person
against a display* that wears the pants.   (*an absence)
Too soon to kill insightful stumbles
not going to lie it doesn't look good

to span the fun of centuries
and never feel about anyone
talk to you a second?
The wound is a bad man.

A Long Home

Catch that crowd falling
so slide to see sky

no fuss as clouds fall back
cold hands caught, dismissed

body again folded under
what is it, toasty? I want

you to want it. Scatter.
In fact some skipped their hives

to lead more treacherous dogs
among churches, woodsheds, caves

or places to be touched
by your attention leaving

this railroad has no trains.

Pirate Video

If there's no handle to stun a grab
mutual rebate, late night desperation flicks
close the door to outside
instead of escaping the basement.
One falls back to know so well
the measured degree of difficult walks
floor to floor, cut down visit
to the ten cent store.
Have you been loved that way before?
Lost in a substantial ticket
just that close to the fiddled window?

Empty Station

For the time being he's
charged as a juvenile time warp. Give us this last
look at who's been going around

one belly up burden a little hostile.
Get your own possum. Anything can turn
the morning into production units

without a second opinion. Furnish a room
with a ceiling of sky like the ad
has a sale on now. With all these knives

and flashbacks around, think fit,
look lucky, wear random obliterated
half eaten boxes of love. Stop that love

before it gets described. Not for another
paid piper. Real personal questions can be
readily implanted. As many times

as one time counts down like a huge
life-altering thing, we could surface,
dig, flail independent of bodies

labeled with names. I knew that?
Alternatives might appear in a bet
about who gets left at the crossroads.

Man As Dog

Try floating
to let distance

guide the stopped
overflow touch

missing. No one
denies the force

reflection haggard
weave. Stub

or super stub
in gummed up

top down
gab field feds.

Who's fined?
What's fold?

Bit to hire
a lawyer's cut

off actual
pride, displaced

wry sprees
like to lose

the tips to charge
for free. How

to slip all this
uphill to cost

you've never
heard of hearing?

I got this bite
to bite again.

Ordery Aisles

We always launch surprise attacks
blamed loosely that way;

stay tuned to slander
the scarred lens. Fortune's reverse

hangs on to your burger
and strikes out dull nights

with juicy centers, fantastic fruit
a giant supermarket of stalling

may I buy you boneless?
It's just the thing to sting.

Friends sent running fierce
say they're angry, say they're mean

with break and feather, cut
sidemarks and sweeping

in one small rented room.
Let's make do with what's available

gurgling down the occasional glances
washed up on a work day coast.

Gone To Ground

Static bombast in a flower waste
what you're having? Much shirt of dissolve
flounders squeeze play.

Why downtown stadiums hardball.
Flushed back. Stratified over a basin
to have but not to hold. Doesn't

muck mean to do the bookend.
Stable table. That stack would ask
to happen again, flourish expertise

upon esteemed drubbings. What did
honey turn to true sweets or plural.
Two runs propel keys.

That's no way to pull down the shelf
church of the row forlorn brit popsicle.
Ask me over easy.

Language and culture course health
drunken valet cleaners. Rid of
fast easy hair euphorically. Charm.

Entirely not to seek as plenty.
Together in cheese demise club beats.
Get into a zone and foggy.

So Bad As You Say

What's a little mid-life critique
doubling as a cash dementia

incinerated fabric hunt, long time telling
to get tattooed as the boss of you

thought of as you, untold
support system bathroom chatter

licking the silverware clear
when it's almost time for cake

after random shootings,
clothes ripped off at an inappropriate

joke about two plumbers in a tub
and get a new face at the lost and found

more for the money, my zesty omelette
don't you know I'll treat you

in the ticket? Am I supposed to sing
once more for people who've gone?

Counting Pertinent Criticisms

Don't make me come down there
and kick your Wall Street butts.
Check out all the sexy hysteria
the blue moon service will be okay

hi, it's easy to abuse the phone.
Describe the new as good, caught
in one small public presentation
that leaves out then leaves. Never

let it settle? Hang on a second,
Pickett. Is it time to get back
in the reparations game? Dinner with dancing
flame accidents, will these stitches

hold back what's left of us?
You only knew me generically
while people's heads bobbed past, fragrances
that turn to fuels. This is your brain

after snorting competing commands
shooting faster than theories of speed.
Why'd you want to move in here
next to officially sanctioned targets?

Please Out The Proper Forms

The rest of the rats on a heap.
Trips on glass, startled refuge
drops off, pulling digests down

where one might fall away some more
dying or not living clatter
if scripts can kill the players off

and now you. Meaningless redundance, again,
maneuvers to gain the proper authority
driving night and day, flesh for rebate

when the foibles of evil descended
on Champion City. Who's naked now?
Parking's short at the mall.

Or we could spin where cars never go
and no one counts the number of romps
not found in top drawers, only one growl

to label who wants to be president.
In the future see the schedule
of crisp green stuff, not just germs

but a bold new artificial energy
we dare you to compare. Jointed options,
downtown roughed over, the problem's fine

as a friend and as a stage play.
Anyone else gets on that elevator
there won't be room to ride to the sky.

Mantra

Don't do drugs
don't fall in love

don't go to work etc.

Pardon My Romanticism

Evaporation works the machine
in a good mood. Jaunty day of the word
keeps no wind, the street at noon

gets fired for everything, lipstick on teeth,
left and right in the business. You've become cab driver
number two, drive the blasted heat

to porcelain safaris, another route
to make nothing happen. Is terror gone
in basic hydrating? Feistier than before

this one fits the display
of insurance to go, killed off my character
find it see it hide it away

at the scratch for life cast off
middle of the blue. I feel like skating
all the way to the night's last flight.

Caught

You've called back space laws
and find you guilty. Double

TV sonic overdubbed Batman,
after suffering a border attack,

coins the rackets, critiques,
drives another toll pickup

wishing for a nickel. I'm going down.
You're accused of murder.

Private Search

Do a tiny investigative
lack in the universe

to touch as bodies
called you and me and them

discovered to treat
as others mistreated

might be our only chance
for hours slurped down

difficult to trouble
one multiple inundation

to leave the kiss
open everywhere

more real than Friday
ignores what could be

Philosophy As Goodbye

Aware to still be talking after
ends would decide to begin again
where separate learning moves away
so one can see. How did we

pass on. Who got caught
in the person one sees oneself reflecting
past talk one fakes as a future
temple over the highway, space display

of getting lost on belief in thought's
advancement standard achievement deceptions
to be outside one's inside twist
broken in half. There was never any place

final melded both, here on ice
to bind it. It had the nail.
I sat on the square and looked around.
More was there than I'd been hid from.

Thanks For Having Me Out

Ever rescued a burning building
or one more slide away from a play
to read your lips? Maybe they'll name

yours after you. Good with weird things
or doubled through an astonished audience
that's predicted years of lights gone dark

picture here, picture there, how to say
begin tonight tomorrow's goodbye
like a brilliant must-see. It doesn't work

to weld to any other background
fear might fit better. Just imagining
how you'd catch the bouquet?

I don't think we should promote the stars
we tell our friends about on benders
so spun they seem a standard sudden

way to count the skulls on walls
one could marry into. Welcome to no one
like no one you've ever been welcome

to fall. Quickly, what was issued
to carry? As long as we're having fun,
let's wonder why it's fun we're having?

Who's There?

For Mi Yeun

There's your real name that's secret
and the public one you hate

when you ask me what I call myself
in order to fake a traditional ritual

stuffed with gifts we both can't use.
It's time to miss each trick more often

and wave goodbye to nice little walls
and insubstantial claims. The confession,

the reaction. An all new get real.
Remember the compliments when we stole gold

or followed long dead rules? The ring is gone
given the history. I lied to my best projection.

Maybe the miscue becomes irreplaceable
when we can't call cops or the company

and sit here drifting in a corner
sterilized once a week. Another adventure

in every bowl, so comfortable they're not there,
doctors as artists as people we trust

keep getting funnier, trading for chances.
Who's it time to impersonate now.

Today At Eleven

Every arena organized so we kiss
under someone else's sense
fury retreads. Poorly equipped for midwinter,
I want you never inside
the world's blandest emerald scheme. Rocket
empty thoughts hound to love
the final rates possible, play with me
smeared all over the abyss
taking another job. Of all the slanderous
looking for people drifting apart,
we dropped the tank, the tangled furor
dog on the block. The scripts
come to my house and I'm killed
for a fun time deal. How many
crackpot laminated spinoffs
ramble the parkway? Lost a lot,
glad to be along, or picked at
soothing weaves in a small number
of insulated cases. The beacon sure lights
these small city no doubt sandbars.

Art Imitates Art

I saw this in a movie once:
take the ultimate eavesdropper
apart on a pin, first contestants

labeled friends saying you're
not hopeless, there's my favorite
addiction called back for the week

and sent the little general in
to get the part of the guy in the cab
when there's no handy hardware

displaced on ridicule. I'll be there
settling into an awkward night
of one who's doubled like a spare

morning and later that morning
too bad there's not any more us
to throw any other ground to the ground.

Scorecard

Rambled into mistaken racing
we're not having birthday blues, rough scratched displays
no more who shows up

the occasional menu, so basically
pull pieces to the pit. Laundered
feed drones distribute rebuttal

to dismay, what would you do?
Now it's cold in the living room.
Staging the surreptitious encounter

fells no normal lash surprise
with no idea. Food and drink
for poets and spies, cash lease men,

trundled feet under a solid
tapped out switch. You have plans,
a clever spoof vis a vis

big things. More control more headroom.
Keep the pit bull occupied?
I'm the cap who pushes the caps

until you hear them click, starting
markers out. Create a diversion.
Next as in nowhere, stay clear.

Shifting

Questions, remember? Dusted
for prints of sincere attacks

call me how a cast of names
sullen against the usual backdrops

never stop a slip in starship colors
one has to die and die on.

Now's no time to stall a tangle
among the melancholy horns

or refuse to darken a window.
Freedom is the solitude to pay for?

The day reflects another mouth
and substantial nightfall fabrications

mean anything to be out
of the life they're talking past

and say you still owe them.
So you call up crying

that it would be good to have it back
when you see me dead on the six o-clock news.

Resplendent Rituals

Try this new screening slip
to see if anyone lives here now.
In all these little walks around
what do you sense about last laughs

for faces in hands, let's meet
until we don't know who we are.
Who's the stranger at the table
telling us how to sleep on through

and wander down to a random vista.
We can always afford here and there
chop chop, throne and visitation
more than the cost of a concept.

Note the famous chickens on wheels
have got the goods that others came for.
Still it's good to not be lost
in the lined up echo, eye for gorgeous

occasional thrills at the station
and dreaming how to catch the air
when phone calls try to poll us;
I'd like to take that to go in the morning.

Can I Have That Addiction?

While you're working you're playing
long lasting energy paste to swallow
a spectacle back together while faults

spread out in dependable curves.
The body is fighting itself.
What to say about extra torque

crammed into a demanding public?
Could we call this stir a melt down
evaluation period, hope displaced

on underhand service subtly competitive
or making frantic displays on bridges?
Venus and Mars resist a theory

of fortune, grunt on the return.
Telling it to jelly here
the old bed routine, not too happy

adjusting wobble in price-scaled legs.
Toss the top straight out the window
or trade it for an exhausted ambivalence.

The Tapeworm Was Her Soul

for Dan Gutstein

I loathed nature during
the gossip in Milan, religious journey speaker
makes identity union. Vexation and torment,
I drive big ones, my mouth feels wet

when I thoughtfully eye the action in Gunsmoke
as though it were a cow. Did my soul tell me
I was an idiot? A good bone structure,
my new great mystery stands before me

remote as an animal. On reconnaissance
to the House of Pancakes, a chirpy lavender scent
wounded my neck. Heaven is a bed
of emergency Budweiser? It's an honor

to introduce my favorite professor
and his burning heart. Don't worry,
I know you're dead, but tonight,
raw by dawn and in a festive mood,

turn your face towards me. Humiliation, rage,
therapeutic use of commitment, lives,
dilemmas, contexts, the yoke. Three generations
transform the Iowa Writer's Workshop.

He who chose at last is chosen
and sometimes feels like a girl. Their behavior
was circumspect, put food in my mouth.
She took lethal poison and then she was dead.

Who Declared The Drought?

All out of gone to breathe
may split beneath apart compartments.
What's the moment before

technically nowhere to be
not like it hasn't been done
and dropped? You'd wait

for some blown set of closing
major door to door
combustible drafts? The face

against the face puts rough
and soft touch to erase
every stripe marshaled to salute

a grasp long unknown.
Jump it right now.
Slip off the bus

and walk around, hands
to lock, scrabble and wring
a gasp in flammable air.

Left Back Twice

Blacked out block on a turnpike block
looks like an action star, coming soon
unleashing a monstrous force while we're
hanging the time to come home again. At a price

that's un-New York. Who'll hammer
half hours crashing in on chaos
to rent cruel intentions. Guaranteed
to protect all valuables weirdly

saying yes to a pipe, not the other
way uptown, I don't own
the stock with my initials, do you?
I keep getting signs to see my father.

At the rotisserie, spinning chicken
might seem an omen anointing America's
newest tired intimacy, burnt at the stake,
three friends winding up in impossible

love postures. What just happened?
The joke is that you took the hat
to cheer yourself up. The interview bit.
Here's one hundred twenty-seven dollars.

Shoulder Over

I'll tell no more to backwards
or fall over traffic dementia

don't toy with toys as pick you up?
Before I go where anyone needs

avert eyes, local restaurant chain of command
somehow went through five replacements

faking dumpsters in Connecticut.
I don't know, why don't you taste it

or call it cake, lending a runner
towards a lostness coming close

and one of us could get amnesia?
What's so strange about riding away?

Lives, Impersonal

Clank slates rumble a pace
don't miss the bed on the ramp
how self-involved are current involvements?

What's this plastic over the century?
Don't want brains dragged
through the chain deli? It's okay

to compete for tools? Our alignment
tilts. No one wants renter's
insufferable bills at a time

to screw over the roles. Don't let
the snooze car sign for you
under the king's crown. More and more

residents find it hard to breathe.
In a world of some bodies
any star resembles a star

while pulling up to mutual stops.
I wonder whose rate is going lower
than closed caption considerations

for good lives at great prices
hey, watch it! It's you and a game
like every game you've ever played.

No One Has Any Excess Qualities

while reading Robert Musil

At the new partial construction deliverance,
fading out requires a pattern,
feeds a bomb to self-worth erosion
that can't find a comfortable mirror

when the city blacks out. Who are you
trapped under this time? Mention
the durable metals, European cheeses
and other widgets made by the hour

and by the hour. "You can't treat me
like one of your discarded jokers,"
the engineer said to the hazy backdrop.
In a time when young intellectuals

scavenge for scraps of would-be genius,
why be surprised you've learned to sell
like a history of credit? Have there been better
reasons to laugh between memos

that laid us out in the punch line?
It's almost time to be free
of any single direction, proclaim the end
of wage work, lack, and theory.

Daily Masks

For Jeff Hansen

Yes it was him okay it was me
no place to hide our gambling convictions
in the lost room. Do you have

any thoughts on being stuck in the tunnel
buy a building, kill a bug,
stare down the barrel of the wind,

eat in? That's what happened
and there's more. What phrase implies
the local lingo? Hello, friend,

we've gone down and back again
like ruthless people on steroids
it's not a critical time right now

to top the toughest guy in toy town,
protect the underside of interest,
pick up things for a bureau

that won't change what it claims to.
Did you make that face
or did it make itself on you?

Tour Map

One gap on a redundant space
maybe disperses the level, guy with ferrets
as staggered symbol. Bedroom, bathroom,
living room, questions turn the tale against
my fate alone in a lighthouse
where no one likes the guard to know
how we get it out of our systems
and hit where it hurts. What are you doing
after you can't take anymore?
See near, see far, see what you never
see coming. Punctures instantly.
Some people risk their lives for things
they later forget to notice.
One day when you jump for a bit
of land, it won't be land
you learn to fall from land on.

No One Lives Where They Live Like That

It's far so hard to be bored.
Shall we drive the night to shards?

Where do we hide the sky over faces
one step further than breaking down

to indicate what's dead and serious.
The showroom's the thing. The ensemble

lets no one know. Are we gone yet
into flak reiterated stumbles?

This morning I was in love with condos
resembling an institutional nexus

like a new bump. Rapid clogging throats
suggest we'd rather not be talking.

There's no word to find the fuse
burned down to one way or another

louder than a sound; the total system
shouts back that there's no way to leave.

Closed Angle

Microscope season, one's underneath
and trees and streets and trucks
add up, burrowing a place

to cast its eventual split
and trust this ride of minutes
to throw away what nothing can stop?

Dreamy on the subway, stares
gotta get more dark at rich
loaded let outs, half-priced

or not to see oneself in things.
Secrets on a hidden avenue
will keep a precious little factory

churning through offhand bruises
taught on stairwells, caught at dusk
conveniently and stored.

That must be the time to run?
Fling a scrupulous reciprocity?
Where's mercy sorry no mercy tonight.

How Much Is The Furnished Room?

The afternoon goes dark surreptitious
on an insubstantial agenda
changing the course of tiny
absences making the switch

too easily. We're lighted red
to die all night in intrigue
now, there's more electric
kiss to can the kiss goodbye

as one lonely declaration gets stoned
among strife, waste labels
we were going to sell in France
or otherwise rip off the world.

I want some decimation pronto
taking the time to wind it 'round
an imitation of what got away
and left me drunk in this boat

where current taskmaster countries unite
to light some flame retardant feds
anybody smell something? I just
woke this groggy premonition.

Is This The Dangerous Doorway

Astride another policy dementia
I just want to celebrate, freedom's never
lost easier, who else wants special

invisible detours? That's so weird
said the D.C. cowboy, people just happened
to circulate unfounded rumor

about impure beef. Drinking to forget.
Be on the lookout for anything falling
like a resemblance. Wait. Hello.

Hand Me Down

These last minute turned keys surge
through plugged-in telephone brain waves

with mystery information sharing
it's time to trade for. The big dog ran

off with your initials. Speed dial terminals
happen to shock another face

or slam the door and give the finger
to vulnerable emotional sore spots.

I'll be right with you okay?
I've got to jam this pen in my eye.

A high speed chase that causes confusion
in roles determined by low ticket items

careens right past the Dairy Queen
in places with names. In a day

or two we'll wear the patch
to keep redundant contaminants out

when we try living all over everything
that gets in the way of what got us here,

one more night through sudden streets
to credit refusals of the wrong innuendo.

The Litter Of Exhaustion

Flame bundles available per folks
easy to please, these two stylish schticks
pull theirs, pull ours, cost more

in plastic starter packs
because they're there. Thanks for the get well
bucket of peas, great fragrances

to protect those legs, intimate peaches.
Look, everyone: it's the plug-in
night stand hamper pads with pedals

wearing us out with worry. Let's get rid
of what got rid to be rid of giving
to that big dog and that was no dog.

Slice hurts on the sly. Speed dial on behalf
of the on-call doctor. Now that I'm head
illumination catalog cancer referee,

I get to make the decisions. Switch faces
how much for how long. In the room
the room talks back. Not again,

strapped, waiting to stay for
the duck and the mouse and who's let down
during interactive final farewells.

Or That One

Flocking to the latest spinoff,
eventually the rhythm gets you
good collapses. The play's
pretty great, a fusebox blows

the psyche to bits on infomercials
when told no. So strange, standing there
as an autonomous connection
that could be opened. Maybe the crazy fog

could be the way we missed each other;
two flats slip a sharp. Buy a state
and name it like no one's home
or down again tomorrow. Is that why

the lost guy says there's time to trip
current presentations of style going
fast through the yard? Ready
to void concern? Pull apart

a concept of glory, gambling on future
ostentatious pleasure seekers
selling top times to soar. Stop looking
through the door to the door on the other side.

Kiss My Dandy Machine

The shuttle ropes a set of levers
while meeting rabid fitness goals
now that there's guaranteed great

foolhardy pluck. Are you
kidding the repellant? Further reductions
qualified as rights to play

with dangerous tools that no one knows
about themselves. Pour it all in the blender,
instigated madcap roustabout

starting to snore. Will those bells
let us out of this yard? Drop
the essential section procedures

whispered, bought and sold blunders
listed by the in-house critic.
Now is not that long from now

that two steps on binging bliss
won't reflect on loss that ads
itself to itself in repeatable clashes.

Crossing Signals

Can't seem to agree that our problems are solved,
demographic response incrementals

passed around at a mixer. Interglobal cash
doesn't have to persuade the usual suspects

to raise frosty bad boys. Lost luggage in airports
resembles each day known and loved

by its edges. Flimsy excuses at last check counters
say it's time to talk, keep heading out

to pick a goodbye cover story. The trap falls
so look right into it. For a little sugar

the door kicks back to next quarter figures
dropped off on Blue Street, opening

a new debate that cancels darkness
by suggesting a Central Park picnic.

Available Lotions

End no sender skinning care.
Resorted evaporation, one moment's last
rescinded wreck emotes. Solidified

refusal warlord gives and slides
dropping sharp on the break. Sympathy pain
in one more good game goes

too unbelievably. Harder than nothing
is as it sounds. Twist through the headlines
on the day a personality split

on money and principle. Full trial
speed bender frames, three tragic
stories and the truth about guys.

Row the boat to a bubble. Lighten
the factored consultation, toxic
lambasted high points, logical and early.

Health Industry

Sear an extra bend in the fold
big guys use to make big bucks
only in area theaters, a dealer near you
can undermine the publishing industry

in print and person. Tell me
what you're doing while you do it
in the back room waiting judgement.
No one's here right now to take

us out of the usual bodies or maybe
delay the service. It's a known
way to shake off the mood of clogged
information streaks. Some old trophies,

plaques and badges to clear your head
of suspects not yours to save
could still be left on the curb. Did you hear
the debate about who's getting clobbered

if we drift apart in dreams
of how to avoid the future? The so-called free
star power sneaks up. Can no myth replace
the one of unified empire feelings

sliding on its darkside? That's what the saving
case load can do. Did you lend
your last chance yet? Wholesome whole grains
sure know how to become unwhole.

Management Theory

When looking at the problem there's always
a problem to the side of it
so resembling and looking blends

dragged for blocks against older
divisions of attention. The listeners
gathered to split the shortage dots

between a couple suckers, referee,
innuendo, reputation drain.
Like to fix the tubing rumble?

Sorry we're all out. For every case
a case encased inside it keeps
inscrutable folded misnamed revenge

in three for one dress downs. That's not advice.
It's repeated already started happening
over again, a matter of time before hands

touch where nothing plays. Were we
or not? The talk turns, investigates
the cold in the out in the cold of.

The King Of Comfort

We're going to need a distraction
foreshadowing daily burst illusions

fobbed as love gum down at the mattress
shock room. It makes more sense

throttled in an ensemble backwashed
for everyone you know. Clears throat.

Do it all the time. Blow up
the receipt in an actual answer.

My theme song fractured one
crazy dog park, new collars, leashes,

great party charges. Now as little
as a dime to bring the night home.

I called everyone I know and the curse
is stronger like a funded program

decides to distribute who wakes up.
It seems a perfect time to bow out.

The Audience And The Masterpiece

Hard to believe what death's mistaken
craft word has a wrapping for
when the boy's love makes the rabbit real

after hitting up a couple of dealers.
That's an incredibly meaningful orange.
Money and equipment reneged on short notice,

contract a crossbow, don't work for months,
borrow the keys to a foreign apartment,
dive down, all answers finished without

invoking another universal language.
Are you the accident spokesman?
So I went, I be, acted like a bank

in the mess, crunching. Cleaned up
in the kitchen display, who hates
the unexpected public part?

Let's all go see a musical
drain extravaganza. Spun and refracted,
there's a service in town to fund

giant tears behind glass. Don't recognize
the rebel ripoff? It's about time,
all about it and things that don't exist

outside developmental schemes. How to throw
the garbage out on the garbage ratio
quarantined with a beautiful sidestep.

Omelet

Back from ignoring my prospects
to dream at the airport, quick get the call
that says the status quo remains
uncorresponded tricks at the stoop

over easy flair. Who do you
say to think you are, bubble timed
and still one can be touched so boldly
to flame imagined stuns on up

waiting all day in needless work.
Come out forever, an hour trapped
in the code that doesn't want to be altered
when some get cut to not feel a thing

along the lie in the seam of a gift
to tell how one balks at one.
We'll have this faraway clamor hotline
to avoid getting caught on the moon.

Following The Weather

The sign of no perpetual storm
tracks its image system when silence
bristles at a switch. Superstition

plays out its bond, correlates
a rambunctious spark, trembles
on a good sense lie. Did you list

the unexpected connections, look out
from the cost worthy vista? Don't get
too attached to the story told

imploding. As long as a mouth shuts
on having to sacrifice the latest
scale for video police, one piece looks like another

no excuses event on the highway.
When we kept it to ourselves
the world was bound to slip out.

Help Wanted

It's always nice to meet the fans'
jukebox quotidian rotunda. From now on
your name is stop tearing down
glitches in the market. If my circ-

ulation has shooting pains
in an empty house, we'll be
afraid of the dark every day and close
up shop shocked ruts a long way

not nothing no more. Have a hanging
slow magic sensation; that drumming tremor
will consider you shortly. Still going through
deserted theatricals, warden and prisoner

naked on the chopping block. Look around
when the world stops turning; the freshly squeezed
impersonal demands define the level
to turn up under. Maybe someday

we'll get less saver rebounds
and compassionate flybys, so these times
can be compared against perks
on a break. Can you hear me

in backroom rules? Put together again
the last time we resembled a wreck,
it won't do to manufacture
costs getting lost in the singed old niche

or pass along more reality slippage.
Who's ever fought harder to save condemned
ways to choose? There's nothing like
when it'll be better, packaged to go.

Is That Your Recorded Voice?

Flung through
the rebound thrown

down in that
position seeing

work from work.
Maybe that caliber

stolen perpetration
doesn't care if we

put names to slipped
phone call floats.

The modern
unfocused anxious who

fit you? Don't buy
the beauty policy

dry-cleaned thing
without thumbs.

I had no keys
to open a care

burst deal on the claw
impacted clause.

Heard about
the secret special

total lender
as the picture goes up

with you
in it as some

line you never
put up on?

Bingo

With compartments, a rushed blockade
bought things on TV before
organic substances turned up discovered

beneath a dog. Let's work on rebuilding
an honest half-tracked bundle
of right timed other ways

to cover the trail we screamed
on in wax. What happened between walls
became no night to laugh down

so badly not told again.
Just to work it out to want
stories lost before they're told

in a quarter hour alley.
The major issue today is living.
Dent resistant, refurnished friends

blocked out thanks from the body
of nothing that talks about a loss
locked in a long time. How was awful

replaced by a turn out?
Because they'll know we've been listening
I think we better get left in the open

nicked by cash dependent loyalty,
chips taken one at a hundred times
the biggest trap for games to cover.

Road Speck

Who's conducting this close out
loses theirs in subliminal waves
to set our faces crooked down
the big fall. When I put on

my wire this morning, expensive fade tubes
looked deceptively stuffed with traffic jostled
through long suffrage hostage wars
married in a contradictory winter. Candles, champagne

laid out in this lifetime.
It started when we ripped each other up.
Soon we'll find ourselves in the car
unsettled as collapse on the screen

sulks like a pseudo-innocent victim.
Now with newly discovered footage
squad hopped on a scraped clear window
in a corner lease. Plenty of people

helping on the interstate strap were shot
out to a magical misunderstanding. Why don't you
stamp valid on your answering flap
gruesomely dodging what nobody knows.

Look The Other Way Again

Give it a name-wracked rap
suspicious about stuff
until the shot moves further away

to play for thirty replies
where the wall comes clear. A room
a man leaves, a woman avoids

both too sure to spin. That's no way
to introduce the family dementia
chasing itself around the city

face to face. No one respects
the bucket. No one goes totally back
to how weird it ever was;

we're drowning tomorrow's trades
today. Go unhook the smoke
you paid you never did for.

When did silence happen fairly?
We are not a space to fall in.
Move to a less high profile spot.

Little Love Games

Why not hire the pause
umbrage maneuver, decision maker
who nods along without knowing

at the kid's table. Never mind the electrical
shriek. I don't get it, have no faith
in the final chance to turn down

half a loaf that's better than none.
Want some loss on that disruption?
Door locked, swear you won't tell

about the daily emotional traps
having a bland resurgence. Like your job,
money man? The same well known labels

reject the way you look in the boss'
speed buzz. The key to the cuffs
could scoot on down the chute a moment

and the facts that jeopardized the star
four quarter calculated fright fests
will make something up; they're good at lying.

Nothing Rhymes With Release

Trappings reigned,
essential advancement fabric

stuck in mouth,
your personal best

recapped at their mercy
in Poughkeepsie. Told me

how to end
up face down, trip first,

rugged pockets replaced.
Can you love

candor committed
at the family table, keep

leaving gone
world wrong flung

given at the usual
hash holy hound?

Tame the taken
stuck sharp strain

doing anything
to make day quit.

Direct fare
don't get no one there.

Feeling In Touch With My Gettings

Cheerfully competitive, handling the hot potato
every time the time turns 'round
to understand how long the seasoned
recognition replaces our will

on a big board. Congratulations
on reveling on the jury, baby, spied
like a gem. Garage.
We're actually going to be set up

in a problem great to love two cents
did I miss something? So many lines
to learn so fast, remember the next
one forgetting morning, taking a walk.

How far away can an aura go
lying on the table in front of a screen
where two people kiss or pass the flu
to a big job in my father's house

naked and playing an instrument.
Don't you love to spin like that
too sick to be sick, serving sauce with attitude
adjustment extravaganzas, the whole nine lives

mortgaged for a buckle. Was it alone?
One world and more malevolence.
Look at the imitation as flattering
the flaks who'd like to be to blame

for hanging around. I want to see everything.
Who planned and planned and planned?
Who took the person inside their head
to watch the boats escape the harbor

while thinking there might be more?
Keep the hair you have, okay?
Wish it on the final act, living better
in the beholder whirling the wall.

Spite Club

Anyone want to enjoin me
in the snake room? There's nothing
like a cool click rotunda

lethargic after feeding.
Commit to the moment
picked up left off

reasoning. Stop.
This is a terrible actor
badness paint up

mud flung miscue
with what? If the scene
had more artificial heat

top of the line tangle
tough place designed
to take it. The most solid

well built buckle under
released for sneaks. Blown
and plundered early

back and forth fun
again sometime. Nice
to meet you goodnight.

Reversed Charges

Every letdown
costs an over arm

all design scheme,
liquid smooth

made to work for you.
The meat gets cooked

too sad and dreamy
face paper faded

oh! it's beautiful
to play with loss

built on radioactive
hints in doorways

sure, what's on
the awkward tingle

in the house of no
imagination, toss under

the talking props
so long, too deep

it speaks today
nothing like any

fall down dark
puts itself straight through.

Resurrection At The Credit Union

Like two idiots in love
coherence and contradiction forgive
the silence everything else has become

when we choose what moves away
because it can't stand to be in the room
with other losses it's invoked

like friends we know we never had. If I promise
never again to see tonight
as part of work as its own reward,

will I be allowed to leave the drama
during the telethon conversion
through telephones that eat me up

when decisions are made to be made?
Ask again later? Earn a better place
in the central obfuscation debate?

Put the blank streak on the main
reasons to be poor once more
in the quest of insubstantial poems

raining on a check. I could never
forget to see forever in a moment
that kills the chance to speak together.

Paranoia's Revenge

I've not fled a rat trap convenient
to blur we're doing it all again
afternoons no one fears exactly
but falls by the flat side anyway

silent partners depend, operations at risk
of no friends more than professional wheels
while your famous luck has just run out,
a cost to staying afloat on fumes

as the end of what we've built.
You'll defend our right to live this way?
Captured under mistake control?
Go today to make through doors

the acid test of delusional therapy
wilting under a pseudonym, burned
by touching the official picture.
I hear you've been writing poetry lostly

in timed debentures termed refusal
and many local zeppelin robberies
until you've flown so far so fast
that death looks like a machine with wings.

Cement By The Water

Interrupt the calm of the death-like
eager scourge to lose everything

bikes pass, bench or standard silence
on a cloudy Lake Michigan throwaway effort

to think that doing would ever be knowing
obsession of a masquerade

I'm downwind and down. Calling again
for a slice of the latest slice?

Watching more than boats that vanish,
eyes could dream evaporated

on the cliff this town has taken.
No one's either time or a subject

but moved along by hounded training
hands could catch the sky to darkness.

Says see I'm loved and death won't take?
Say no grasp or the face disappears?

Never to be so close by the lake
or vast a burn of thunders

as one more day forgets each self
to clutch that no one runs together.

What Can't Be

For Joanne, in memory of Joey and Hillary

Startled parts in a last embrace
start at daily funerals, giving up
no one thrown along for the ride
years in tearing apart. There's no gestapo
polling feelings about random death
yet each one slips to nothing fast
reported on the hour. Who's got a sleeping
fear of drowning? Not a last chance
for a chance to time the perfect passing
among what must be done tomorrow
to let the orders split up hands
we'll never touch together for.
It's not to go down easily.
Pick again where silence comes back
in between your voice as voices
you remember in starting over
on a day like a day you can't be in
but are, once more, despite who's gone
to leave you here to be leaving, here.

Debt Collection

If the sun could be warm like this on a day
with no hidden nervous tremor
like another bucket of cash
goes to arrange the picture as usual

combustible ways wander away
from projections of selves on things.
I'd like to go where going goes.
Or slanting downwind, dismaying the mess

tossed around by some guy at a desk
trading old futures for one back pocket
bad deal gone bad. When did love
become a dilemma any more than it was

hard to breathe when the air's this clear?
When would we be selling that one?
This day could be about today, leisurely and bright,
if the days weren't stacked like nights inside it.

Making A Break Of It

Connect the interior
childhood cut-up

kick back inundation
leftover dark patch

upon dark seas, caught
in a test drive production

shiny and resilient
go to school, job that's cool

found underneath.
Here's my info.

Friends drop down
the most wanted list

spectacle no one
watches disintegrate.

Could you sign please
to take right apart

and fall on the sidewalk
freeze, you're busted

to cancel chance
that looks good falling

like impersonated death
drunk with power.

Not No More

Having the best head in the sand
to not go twisting insubstantial
I need to remember desolate

out of town night dogs, breaking and entering
to do small chores against icy streets,
forgiveness wrecked on a heave.

Infinite Loop

Sold to a generous misunderstanding
stuck on how to clear the glacier-
like refusal to avoid advancement
criteria full of ammunition

all chaotic and twirly, as far as night's
concerned to toss the haul as dread
in front of the entire. I had it
this morning in the kitchen

messing up the one job to do.
Riding high on disrespect
defended by the warring parties, do we have
the taste for drills all drilled

to lend a hand in the labyrinth?
That's not much money to lose your life for.
Give thanks each day for the little harmonica
hidden in an offstage hour; who knew

we'd have no say in the phrases
that misreport the show? Hot wheels blur
the convention center and no one
trusts anyone anymore anywhere

according to the dominant electoral
pre-determined money. It was simple
to never think that here would be
so much as a small denial

clamps down on its piece. Shall we play
with the disinfected surgical instruments
or the history of conquest divided by region
during the blow off we could never resist?

Some Chairs And A Table

When the house is a wall as so much bound
jutting, no one says how not to turn
too far or stumbled weave, have a broken
office view broken by trees, schedule
effective as go is nowhere, will be open
when a surge makes the plug responsible.
A further jolt wants you the talent
tendered displace, nothing about it
leaks attendance off the stairs.
One could be dumb and diminished, having scored
cleaner than dishes brought round
food of who became rich. Feast infest
comparisons with Silicon Valley, one little
less than loose, hover board interior
says simply there's no me. Drops under.
If we pinpoint schizophrenia genes
or lashed pants in corners, what might it mean
when all around us splits to fifths?
Have you blended one no feeling purgatory
upon an organized swell? Concealed weapons
of uncertain duration to evolve as years?

'Cause I Will And Won't And Would And Will

Skateboarders jump the empty fountain
looks like I'm back on the grid again
no too fat chance to still the breath

caught against a frame. Who knows
the way home on leased perhaps
fumbled, laughing at the glass

among one less substantial glow
defined by buses at stop lights
and people's sudden "oh my God"s

flirting with survival. What next
statue goes up, name of some
guy who owns some gratefulness

did you see me walking
there and grin? Surely the day would flow
along itself to the end of a thought

pressed in an unsuspecting moment
and make me the center of falling.
Grind ahead and perch by streetlights,

all precarious instants of freedom
defined as such and looked right through,
a song, you know, the one not heard

or sung or stored in a storage lock
fractured by betrayal. Do you know the shambles
stranded, hounded towards a ledge

jumped off a dollar a ride to fly
back where we were, startled shift
and a bell rung time was up?

Labored Breathing

Who needs an actual
instigation filter misnamed

night and time
room on the other side

yes, freedom
except for this arm

one fluid quick
roll to floor, stamina

starts Friday
with wall options,

light the dim
understated sidebar

praise of the automotive
press, this just in—

ocean flavor cruise
tender in a bucket

universal soldier
new breed of fighting

here's my binoculars
the log I kept

not even a little
help for it

why this is crazy
jammed subway ache

A Salesman Has Himself To Sell

Con sharping on the lot
requesting release, why aren't we dressed
for the nickel plated reverse display
once we're what we wish for

in second chances, timed consideration
vanishing rapidly. Nervous about
unexpected dissolution, too little love
on a little raft? The world is bigger

darkness than in dreams in darkness
we agreed not to say. No one goes
too far across. Yet in the night
it's cool and we pretend to hold

pretending, holding. Welcome back
to the clear and lost alternative
unlistening and no one leaves
without unfolding forgotten drifts.

Have we gone the wrong way more
than the right way could call the wrong
upheaval? Who's sparing what they own?
What can I do to show you how much?

What Thinks To Stop From Suffering

The phone has rung
my head's a bell

to slow it fast?
Can't have too much morning.

The home's a house
with one last pickle,

body's boarded up.
Push me through a fickle door

to lock behind when gone
astray and drifting under.

You're Around The World, I'm Right Here

Riding the bus yesterday, I caught
somebody's neurosis. Cold, hard,
unyielding, this daredevil game

falls high on the let up.
I'll save my trick right now,
spun on feedback, have to go,

one moment as a bite to eat
in a place on a block, okay then.
That beeping in the hallway

reminds the night which piece to throw
on the fire, up to date bionic features
thinking they're funny. At the lecture,

it's not the lecture I mind,
rubric drop down lieutenant
time bomb mishmash. Obviously

I want to. Playing together was the most
playing I ever had as the most
not much light to change the postures

behaving in the lot. See your dealer
adjusted calculations, maybe the work
will be taken apart from beginning to slip

so pretty on providing slips.
We could count the number of flaws
or go on again in the morning.

EDGE BOOKS

INTEGRITY & DRAMATIC LIFE Anselm Berrigan $10
SOME NOTES ON MY PROGRAMMING Anselm Berrigan $15
ZERO STAR HOTEL Anselm Berrrigan $15
THEY BEAT ME OVER THE HEAD WITH A SACK Anselm Berrigan $5
CIPHER/CIVILIAN Leslie Bumstead $14
COMP. Kevin Davies $15
THE GOLDEN AGE OF PARAPHERNALIA Kevin Davies *forthcoming 2008* $15
AMERICAN WHATEVER Tim Davis $12
THE JULIA SET Jean Donnelly $4
LADIES LOVE OUTLAWS Buck Downs $6
MARIJUANA SOFTDRINK Buck Downs $11
CLEARING WITHOUT REVERSAL Cathy Eisenhower *forthcoming 2008* $14
METROPOLIS 16-20 Rob Fitterman $5
METROPOLIS XXX: THE DECLINE & FALL OF THE ROMAN EMPIRE
Rob Fitterman $12
WORLD PREFIX Harrison Fisher $6
DOVECOTE Heather Fuller $14
PERHAPS THIS IS A RESCUE FANTASY Heather Fuller $14
NON/FICTION Dan Gutstein forthcoming 2008 $14
SIGHT Lyn Hejinian and Leslie Scalapino $15
LATE JULY Gretchen Johnsen $3
ASBESTOS Wayne Kline $6
BREATHALYZER K. Silem Mohammad $14
THE SENSE RECORD Jennifer Moxley $14
THE BEGINNING OF BEAUTY PART ONE Mel Nichols $10
DAY POEMS Mel Nichols $5
STEPPING RAZOR A.L. Nielsen $9
ACE Tom Raworth $12
CALLER AND OTHER PIECES Tom Raworth $12.50
ERRATA 5UITE Joan Retallack $14
DOGS Phyllis Rosenzweig $5
INTERVAL Kaia Sand $14
ON YOUR KNEES, CITIZEN: A COLLECTION OF "PRAYERS" FOR THE "PUBLIC"
[SCHOOLS] Rod Smith, Lee Ann Brown, Mark Wallace, eds. $6
CROW Rod Smith, Leslie Bumstead, eds. $6
CUSPS Chris Stroffolino $2.50
HAZE: ESSAYS POEMS PROSE Mark Wallace $14
NOTHING HAPPENED AND BESIDES I WASN'T THERE Mark Wallace $9.50

AERIAL MAGAZINE
(edited by Rod Smith)
AERIAL 10: LYN HEJINIAN co-edited by Jen Hofer *forthcoming 2008* $16
AERIAL 9: BRUCE ANDREWS $15
AERIAL 8: BARRETT WATTEN $16
AERIAL 6/7: FEATURING JOHN CAGE $15

Literature published by Aerial/Edge is available through Small Press Distribution (www.
spdbooks.org; 1-800-869-7553; orders@spdbooks.org) or from the publisher at PO Box 25642
• Georgetown Station • Washington, DC 20007. When ordering from Aerial/Edge directly, add
$1 postage for individual titles. Two or more titles postpaid. For more information please visit
our website at www.aerialedge.com.